Spotlight on Canada

Bobbie Kalman

A Crabtree Classics Bo

Crabtree Publishing
crabtreebooks.com

Spotlight on my Country

Created by Bobbie Kalman

For Lawrence, Machiko, Alex, Matthew, and Hana, with lots of love. (See p.20)
You all contribute so much to our creative and lively family. We rock!

Author and Editor-in-Chief
Bobbie Kalman

Editor
Robin Johnson

Photo research
Crystal Sikkens

Design
Bobbie Kalman
Katherine Kantor
Robert MacGregor (front cover)

Production coordinator
Katherine Kantor

Special thanks to
Drew Colangelo

Illustrations
Barbara Bedell: back cover, pages 6, 7 (leaves), 11 (pine cone), 15 (Inuit and canoe), 16 (top), 20 (leaves), 29
Antoinette "Cookie" Bortolon: page 20 (flags)
Katherine Kantor: pages 7 (Great Lakes), 14 (bottom), 15 (inukshuk)
Bonna Rouse: pages 11 (flag and leaf), 19, 22, 26
Margaret Amy Salter: pages 14 (top), 15 (box)

Photographs
Lawrence Brissenden: page 20
Confederation Life Gallery of Canadian History: pages 17 (bottom), 18 (bottom)
PBase.com/G. Elliott: page 30 (bottom)
© iStockphoto.com: pages 12, 21 (top), 25 (bottom left)
Robin Johnson: page 27 (bottom right)
Peter Crabtree: page 28 (bottom right)
National Archives of Canada (PA-027013): page 18 (top)
© ShutterStock.com: front cover, pages 1, 3, 5 (top), 6 (left), 9 (bottom), 10 (top left), 11, 13 (all except top left), 15, 17 (top), 19, 21 (bottom), 23, 24, 25 (all except bottom left), 26, 28 (all except bottom right), 29, 30 (top), 31; Elena Elisseeva: back cover, pages 8 (bottom), 9 (top left), 10 (all except top left), 21 (middle), 27 (all except bottom right)
The CRB Foundation Heritage Project/Claude Charlebois: page 16 (bottom)
Other images by Corbis, Digital Stock, Image Club Graphics, and Photodisc

---

Crabtree Publishing

crabtreebooks.com 800-387-7650

In Canada: We acknowledge the financial support of the Government of Canada through the Canada Book Fund for our publishing activities.

Hardcover 978-0-7787-3450-5
Paperback 978-0-7787-3476-5
Ebook (pdf) 978-0-7787-8944-4

Published in Canada
Crabtree Publishing
616 Welland Avenue
St. Catharines, Ontario
L2M 5V6

Published in the United States
Crabtree Publishing
347 Fifth Avenue
Suite 1402-145
New York, NY 10016

Printed in the U.S.A./042025/CP20250325

Library and Archives Canada Cataloguing in Publication
Available at the Library and Archives Canada

Library of Congress Cataloging-in-Publication Data
Available at the Library of Congress

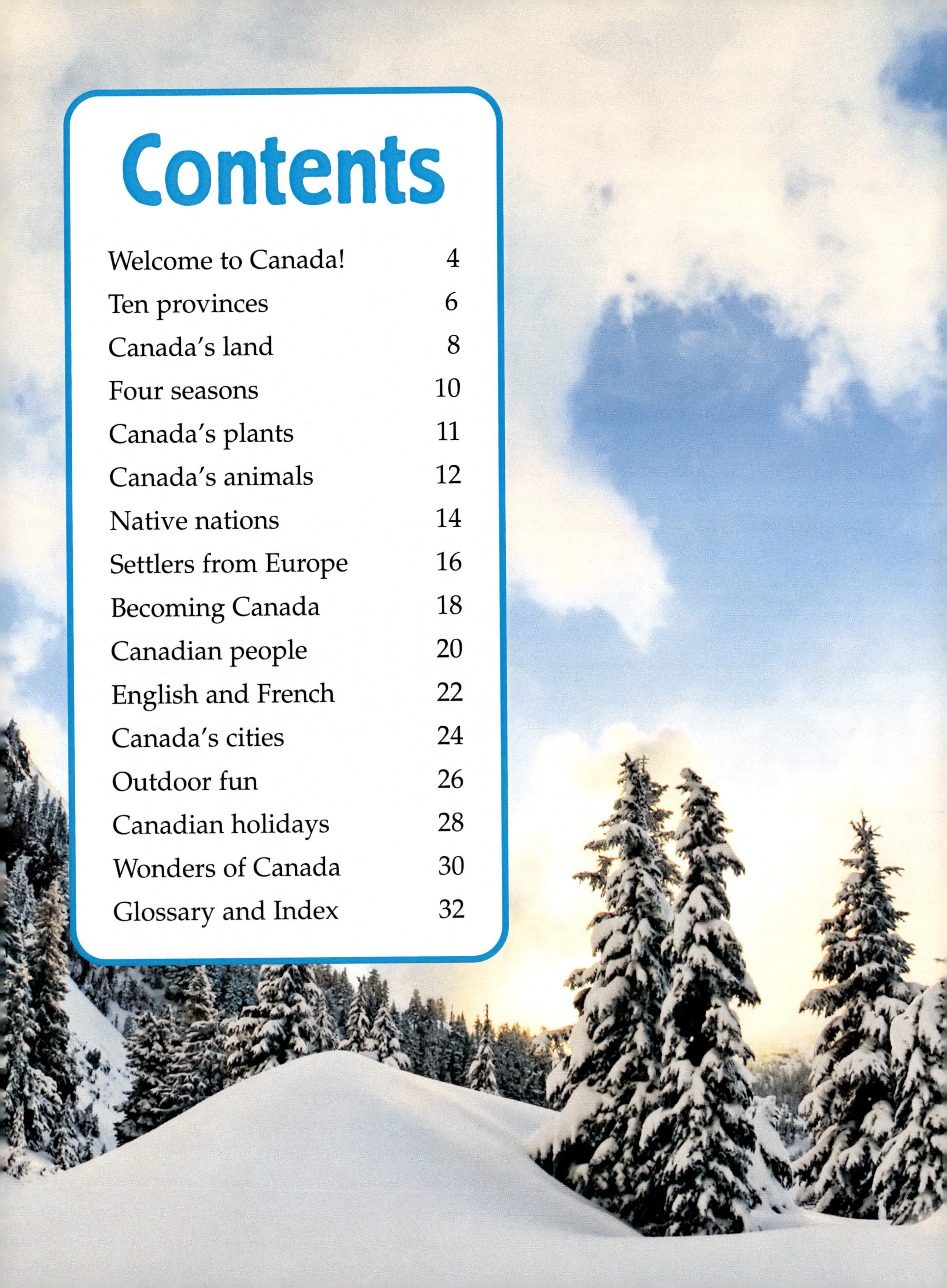

Contents

Welcome to Canada!

Welcome to Canada! Canada is the second-largest **country** in the world. A country is an area of land that has people. It has **laws**, or rules, that the people must follow. A country also has **borders**. Borders separate countries from their neighbors. Canada has only one neighbor. The United States of America is south of Canada. Alaska, which is part of the United States, is northwest of Canada.

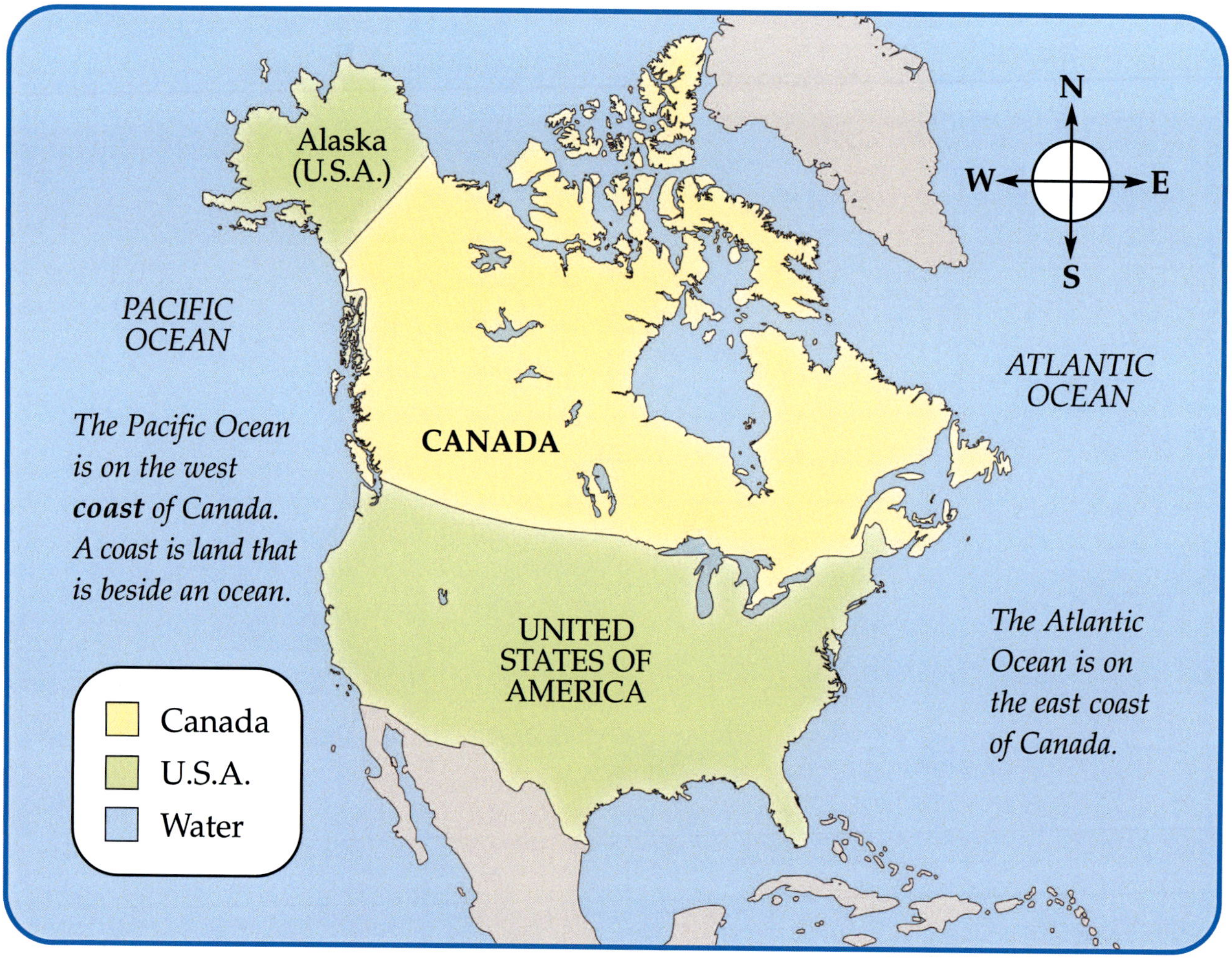

The Pacific Ocean is on the west ***coast*** *of Canada. A coast is land that is beside an ocean.*

The Atlantic Ocean is on the east coast of Canada.

Where on Earth is Canada?

Canada is part of the **continent** of North America. A continent is a huge area of land. There are seven continents on Earth. They are North America, South America, Europe, Asia, Africa, Australia and Oceania, and Antarctica. Find Canada on the map of the world shown below.

Which three oceans touch parts of Canada?
Which continent is across the Atlantic Ocean from Canada?

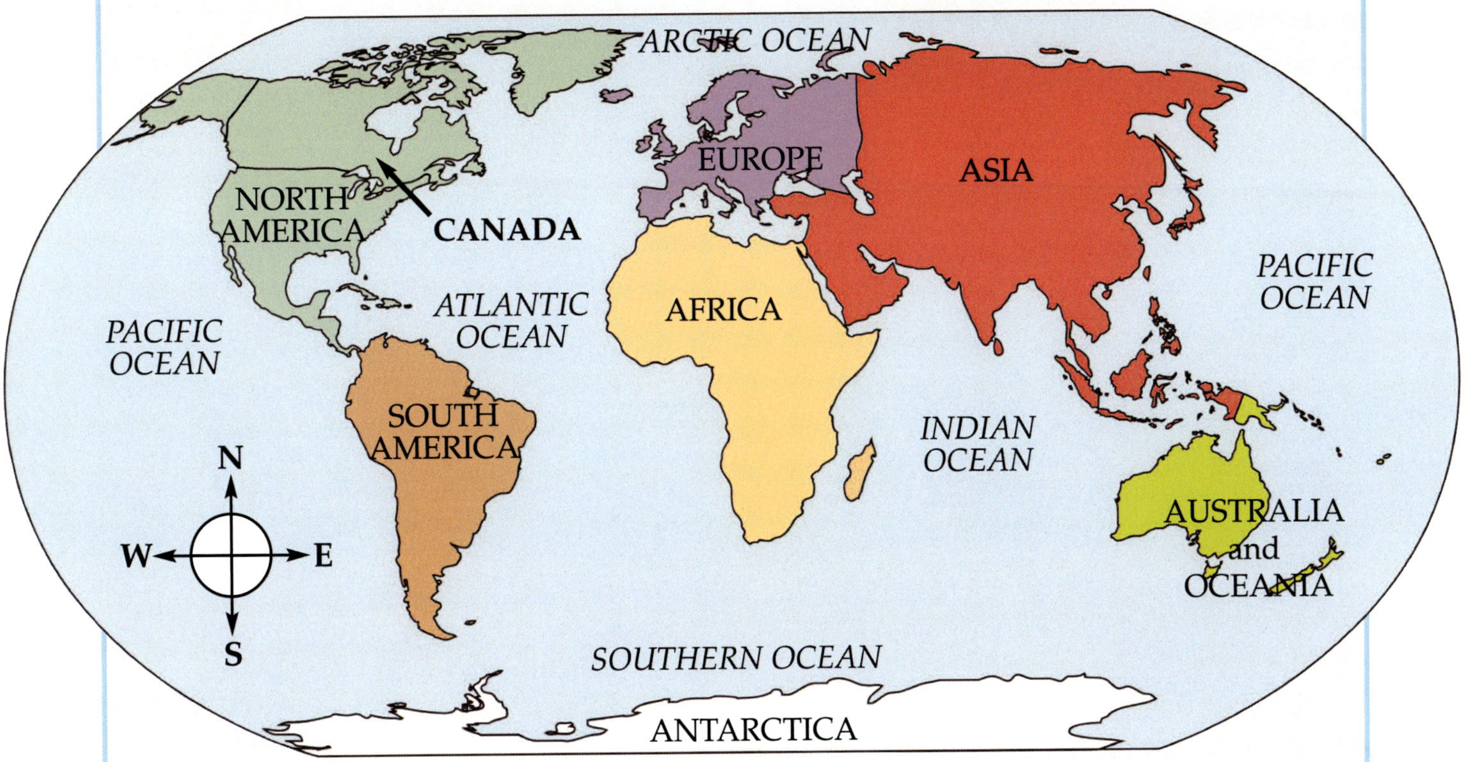

Ten provinces

Canada is made up of ten **provinces** and three **territories**. A province is an area of a country that has its own **government**. A government makes laws and looks after its people. A territory is an area that is run by the country's **federal**, or main, government. Canada's federal government is located in Ottawa. Ottawa is the **capital** of Canada. Each province and territory also has a capital. The government of each province is located in its capital city.

The three territories of Canada are the Northwest Territories, the Yukon, and Nunavut.

The longest river in Canada is the Mackenzie River.

Ottawa is a beautiful city in the Province of Ontario. The Rideau Canal runs through the city.

*The **Great Lakes** are the largest group of **freshwater** lakes in the world. Fresh water has very little salt.*

The names of the Great Lakes are Lake Huron, Lake Ontario, Lake Michigan, Lake Erie, and Lake Superior. To remember them, think of the word HOMES.

***H**uron*
***O**ntario*
***M**ichigan*
***E**rie*
***S**uperior*

Canada has thousands of lakes! It has more fresh water than most other countries have.

The St. Lawrence River connects the Great Lakes to the Atlantic Ocean. It allows large ships to carry goods to and from Canada.

Canada's land

Canada is a beautiful country. It has many **landscapes**. A landscape is how land looks. Canada has thick forests, huge mountains, flat, grassy areas, and some very cold, snowy places. The pictures on these pages show some of Canada's landscapes.

The northern part of Canada is called the Arctic. It is covered with snow and ice for most of the year. Polar bears live in the Arctic.

The land in Ontario and Quebec is good for farming. Grapes, apples, pears, and peaches grow there. This picture shows an apple orchard in Ontario.

Large areas of Canada are rocky and contain ***minerals*** *such as gold, silver, and copper. These areas are part of the* ***Canadian Shield****.*

The Rocky Mountains are found in the provinces of Alberta and British Columbia. Many old forests grow in British Columbia.

The ***Prairies*** *are in Manitoba, Saskatchewan, and parts of Alberta. Prairies are flat, grassy areas of land. Wheat and* ***canola****, shown above, grow there. Canola is used to make cooking oil.*

The Atlantic provinces are Nova Scotia, New Brunswick, Newfoundland and Labrador, and Prince Edward Island. Many people who live in these provinces make their living from fishing.

Four seasons

Some people think that Canada is always freezing cold, but it is not! Most of Canada has four seasons. They are spring, summer, fall, and winter. The **climate** is different in some parts of the country, however. Some parts of Canada are hotter, colder, wetter, or drier than others are.

In spring, flowers bloom in most parts of Canada.

Summers can be hot. Many people go to the beach.

Leaves turn beautiful colors in the fall.

In winter, snow falls in most parts of Canada.

Canada's plants

Many kinds of plants grow in Canada. In spring and summer, flowers bloom and trees grow new leaves. In the fall, many trees, such as maple and oak trees, lose their leaves. Other trees, called **conifers**, do not lose their leaves. The leaves of conifers are sharp needles that stay on the trees, even in winter.

Maple leaf forever

Maple trees grow in every province of Canada. The maple tree is Canada's national plant. The colorful leaf of the maple tree is also a **symbol** of Canada. A symbol is a sign or picture that stands for something else. A maple leaf appears in the middle of the Canadian flag, which is shown above.

Conifers keep their leaves all year.

In summer, beautiful flowers and other plants grow in Canada's Arctic.

Canada's animals

Canada's national animal is the beaver. A long time ago, people came to Canada to trap beavers for their fur. People made hats and coats from the fur.

Many kinds of animals live in different parts of Canada. The animals are suited to their **habitats**, or the natural places where they live. Many animals live in Canada's forests. Some live in or near water. Some animals even live in the freezing Arctic!

Orcas live near the coast of British Columbia. Many gulls and other birds also live there. The orca and the gulls shown above are looking for fish to eat in the ocean.

Wolverines are fierce animals that live in Canada's northern forests. They hunt moose and other large ***prey****.*

Canada geese live in Canada for most of the year. This mother goose is taking care of her ***goslings****, or baby geese.*

Canada lynx also live in northern forests. They hunt animals such as rabbits.

Snowy owls live in the Arctic. Their thick white feathers protect them from the freezing weather.

Black bears and brown bears also live in Canada. These black bears live in a forest.

Native nations

The first people to live in Canada were native peoples. Hundreds of native **nations**, or groups, lived across North America for thousands of years. Each nation had its own language, leaders, and way of life. Some nations were farmers. They grew corn and other foods. Many also hunted animals and caught food in Canada's oceans, rivers, and lakes.

Nations that lived near forests found plenty of animals to hunt, such as turkeys, beavers, and deer.

Some native nations grew corn, beans, and squash. These plants grew well together. Some nations called the plants the "three sisters."

The Inuit made stone statues called **inukshuks**. Inukshuks showed where people had been. They helped guide travelers across the snowy land.

Native people, called Inuit, lived in the Arctic. They hunted seals and whales for food. They used sealskins to make warm clothing.

The Haida lived on Canada's northwest coast. They used cedar trees to make homes and to carve beautiful **totem poles**. Totem poles are tall wooden sculptures. The Haida also built big boats called **canoes**. Some of the canoes could carry many people and goods.

totem pole

The Haida made beautiful works of art, such as this cedar box.

canoe

Settlers from Europe

beaver

The first people from Europe to **settle**, or live, in Canada came from Iceland or Greenland. They settled in Newfoundland for a short time. In later years, people from France and England came to Canada. They came to trade for beaver **pelts**, or furs, with the native people.

French fur traders came to Canada to trade goods for furs. The British also came to set up fur-trading forts, such as the Hudson's Bay Company. Both France and England wanted to control the land.

The Loyalists

The **United Empire Loyalists** were the first large group of English-speaking settlers in Canada. The Loyalists were British people who had been living in what is now the United States. They moved to Canada after the American Revolution, which was won by the Americans in 1781. The Loyalists wanted to remain under British rule.

A Loyalist was a person who continued to support the King of England. The Loyalists fought for Britain.

The Loyalists settled in Nova Scotia, Quebec, and what is now Ontario.

Becoming Canada

*Sir John A. Macdonald was the first **prime minister** of Canada.*

In 1867, the provinces of New Brunswick, Nova Scotia, Quebec, and Ontario **confederated**, or joined together. They became the **Dominion** of Canada. The new country was still under British rule, but it had its own government, as well. Years later, a railroad was built across the country. The railroad allowed Saskatchewan, Manitoba, Alberta, and British Columbia to join the rest of Canada. The last province to become part of Canada was Newfoundland in 1949.

*The men above, who created the country of Canada, are known as the "Fathers of **Confederation**."*

Canada's government works in the Parliament Buildings in Ottawa.

Canada's government

Canada's government is a **parliamentary system**. It is made up of two parts—the **Senate** and the **House of Commons**. Members of the Senate, called **senators**, are chosen by the prime minister. **Members of Parliament** (MPs) are chosen by the people of Canada. They represent the people in the House of Commons. The senators and MPs create and pass laws that all Canadians must obey.

Members of Parliament meet in the House of Commons, shown above.

Canadian people

The **population** of Canada is over 33 million people. Population is the number of people who live in a country. People who live in Canada are called Canadians. Canadians live in a **multicultural** country, or a country made up of many **cultures**. Culture is the way a group of people lives. Canadians have different beliefs, customs, music, food, and celebrations.

These flags are flown on Boys' Day, a tradition celebrated by many Japanese boys in Canada.

This Canadian family is multicultural. The children have Japanese, Hungarian, Swedish, and British backgrounds. They are holding maple leaves to show they are proud to be Canadian.

Who are Canadians?

Canadians do not all look the same. Many have come from other countries. Most Canadians speak English or French, or both. Many people in Canada speak other languages, as well. Canadians are proud of their country and cultures.

These pictures show young Canadians from different backgrounds having fun together.

English and French

English and French are Canada's **official languages**. An official language is used in government and in business. Children also learn both languages at school. These languages came from the British and French people who first settled in Canada.

*The **fleur-de-lis** is Quebec's symbol.*

O Canada

Canada's **national anthem** is "O Canada." A national anthem is a country's song. People sing their national anthem to show they are proud of their country. Here are the words to O Canada in English and in French.

O Canada (English)

O Canada! Our home and native land!
True patriot love
in all thy sons command.
With glowing hearts we see thee rise,
The True North strong and free!
From far and wide, O Canada,
We stand on guard for thee.
God keep our land
Glorious and free!
O Canada, we stand on guard for thee;
O Canada, we stand on guard for thee.

Ô Canada (French)

Ô Canada! Terre de nos aïeux,
Ton front est ceint
de fleurons glorieux!
Car ton bras sait porter l'épée,
Il sait porter la croix!
Ton histoire est une épopée
Des plus brillants exploits.
Et ta valeur,
de foi trempée,
Protégera nos foyers et nos droits;
Protégera nos foyers et nos droits.

English is the main language spoken in most parts of Canada. French is the main language in the Province of Quebec. In Quebec, many newspapers, radio and television shows, and street signs are in French.

The old part of Quebec City looks like it did hundreds of years ago. The streets are made of ***cobblestones****. Cobblestones are small, round stones that were once used to make roads.*

Château Frontenac

Quebec City is one of the oldest cities in North America. A beautiful old hotel called Château Frontenac towers over the city. The hotel opened in 1893 and has become a symbol of Quebec City.

Canada's cities

Canada has many cities. Some are very big. Canada's biggest city is Toronto. It is located in the Province of Ontario. Montreal is another big city. It is in the Province of Quebec. The pictures on these pages show some of Canada's many cities. They are great places to live!

The third-largest city in Canada is Vancouver, British Columbia. Vancouver has been named one of the best cities in the world in which to live. This beautiful city has mountains on one side and the Pacific Ocean on the other. In Vancouver, it hardly ever snows in winter, but it sometimes rains a lot!

Toronto is located on the shores of Lake Ontario. There are many tall buildings in this busy city. The tallest building is the CN Tower.

Montreal is Canada's second-largest city. It is a beautiful city with some very old buildings.

Calgary, Alberta, is famous for the Stampede. The Stampede is a large ***rodeo*** *that lasts for ten days every summer.*

Halifax is located on the Atlantic coast of Nova Scotia. It is called "the gateway to Canada."

Outdoor fun

In winter, many people come to Ottawa to skate on the frozen Rideau Canal.

Canadians love the outdoors! In winter, they enjoy ice-skating or playing hockey on frozen ponds and **canals**. In summer, many people enjoy hiking, camping, and water sports. Canada's national sport is lacrosse. Lacrosse is played by two teams on a field. Lacrosse players use sticks with nets on them, shown below.

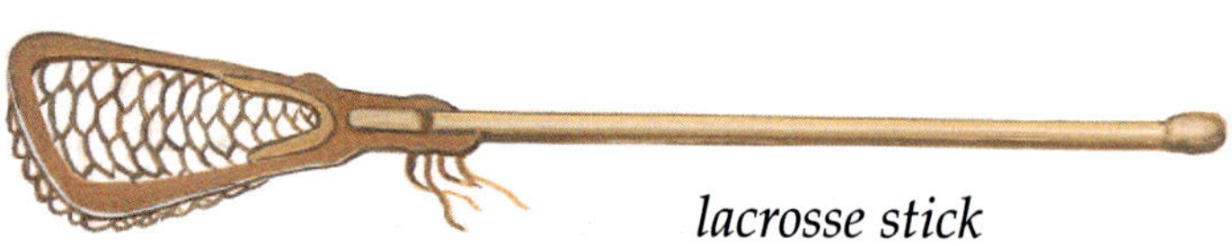

lacrosse stick

Many people spend time in Canadian parks and wilderness areas. Some children learn how to paddle canoes at summer camps.

In winter, many people ski on Canada's huge Rocky Mountains.

In summer, both kids and dogs love to cool off in water!

Many boys and girls play soccer in Canada. They start playing when they are very young!

Canadian holidays

Canadians celebrate many holidays. Some are **national holidays**. National holidays honor Canada and its history. July 1 is **Canada Day**. It was on this day that Canada became a country. Canadians celebrate their country's birthday with parades, barbecues, and fireworks.

On Canada Day, there are fireworks across the country. These fireworks are in the city of Edmonton, Alberta.

Canadians love their country!

In Niagara-on-the-Lake, Ontario, there is a huge birthday cake on Canada Day!

On May 24, Canadians celebrate **Victoria Day**. This holiday honors the birthday of Queen Victoria. Victoria was the Queen of England when Canada was under British rule. Queen Victoria's husband, Prince Albert, brought the tradition of decorating Christmas trees from Germany to England. The tradition, shown right, then came to Canada.

June 24 is Quebec's National Day, or ***Fête nationale***. People all over the province have parades, parties, **bonfires**, and fireworks to celebrate Quebec's French culture. Quebec's flag flies everywhere!

Thanksgiving is celebrated on the second Monday of October. On this day, Canadians enjoy special meals with their families and give thanks for all that they have. Native peoples in Canada began this tradition long ago. Each fall, they held feasts and gave thanks for the autumn **harvest**.

Wonders of Canada

Canada has many natural wonders. They are in different parts of the country. In Ontario, a huge waterfall called Niagara Falls, shown above, is one of the best-known wonders of the world. The name "Niagara" comes from a native word meaning "thundering water."

At Basin Head, Prince Edward Island, there are "singing sands" on the beach. When you walk barefoot on the white sand, the sand makes a squeaking sound! The sand also sounds like a cat's meow if you jab your foot into it! Nobody knows why the sand sings, but it is fun to listen to it!

dinosaur fossil in rock

In Alberta, there is a place where you can find real dinosaurs! It is called Dinosaur Provincial Park. The dinosaurs are not alive. They are buried in the earth and rock. You can see a ***fossil*** *of a dinosaur in the small picture above. A fossil is a mold of where bones used to be.*

Dinosaur Provincial Park also has ***hoodoos****. Hoodoos are rocks shaped by wind and water. They are in areas called* ***badlands****. Badlands are very dry. Few plants grow there.*

In Vancouver, British Columbia, there are huge totem poles that were carved long ago by native peoples. The animals on the totem poles are symbols of native families.

Glossary

Note: Some boldfaced words are defined where they appear in the book.

bonfire A large, outdoor fire around which people gather

canal A narrow, human-made waterway through which boats travel

capital The city in which the government of a country or province is located

climate Weather that has been the same for a long time

Confederation The joining of Canada's provinces to become one country

dominion One of many lands under the rule of one government

government A group of people who are in charge of a country or part of a country

harvest The gathering of foods that have been planted

mineral A non-living substance that is usually found inside rocks

parliamentary system A type of government that has some elected members, as well as a leader who chooses some members

prey An animal that is hunted and eaten by another animal

prime minister The head of the Canadian government

rodeo An event in which riders show their skills with horses and bulls

Index